ACTION ACTION DESPITE THE DISTRACTION!

7 LIFE LESSONS TO
THRIVE & LIVE YOUR DESTINY NOW!!

Dr. Stacie NC Grant

Continue to Stay in Action, love, Dr. Stacie

www.DestinyDesignersUniversity.com

718-525-6184

Book Layout by ShinyRocketDesign

Ordering Information: Quantity sales. Special discounts are available on quantity purchases by corporations, associations, and others. For details, contact the "Special Sales Department" at Info@ DestinyDesignersUniversity.com.

ISBN: 0-9976400 4
ISBN-13: 978-0-9976400-1-4

DEDICATION

We spend so much of our lives seeking to find our purpose. We feel in order to validate our existence we need to find the cure for cancer or be the first person to walk on Mars. *Here is my radical proposition, our purpose is simply to serve God, share His love, and use all our talents to make the world a better place.* Most people are more comfortable with separating the discussion of their FAITH when engaging in business but for me there is no sustainable business without standing in my FAITH! This book is for my fellow #Faithpreneurs determined to LIVE THEIR DESTINY NOW. We refer to our community as #DDUFaithNation and members as #DestinyDesigners.

First, I give honor to God who is the head of my life and for all the great things He has done! I am humbled and grateful to God for bestowing upon me the ability to serve others through His divine inspiration. I am the vessel and He is in CONTROL!! This book is dedicated to my maternal Grandmother, Pernell Agatha Rhoden, my Spiritual Mother, Rev. Mother Cora Paris, and all my collective and communal ancestors (some whose names I may never know) that dared to dream a bigger dream for their future generations than they could for themselves. I am a product of their ingenuity, sacrifice, character, style, faith, and grace.

LOOK UP TO THE HOLY MOUNTAIN

Defeat comes from looking back
Distraction comes from looking around
Discouragement comes from looking down
Deliverance comes from looking up

Rev. Mother Cora Paris

TABLE OF CONTENTS

ACKNOWLEDGMENTS

"Until one is committed, there is hesitancy, the chance to draw back-- Concerning all acts of initiative (and creation), **there is one elementary truth that ignorance of which kills countless ideas and splendid plans: that the moment one definitely commits oneself, then Providence moves too. All sorts of things occur to help one that would never otherwise have occurred. A whole stream of events issues from the decision, raising in one's favor all manner of unforeseen incidents and meetings and material assistance, which no man could have dreamed would have come his way.** *Whatever you can do, or dream you can do, begin it. Boldness has genius, power, and magic in it. Begin it now."*

Goethe

To my "Earth Angels": Andrew, Rebecca, Cassondra, Dominique, Nadeen, Otis, Bart, Felipe, Asia & Karine : THANK YOU! THANK YOU! THANK YOU! for believing in me and pushing me over the finish line. I could not have done this without your time, talent, & service.

STATEMENT OF PURPOSE

Someone very wise once said, *"Life is God's Gift to us and what we do with our life is our gift to God."* Throughout my life's journey, I have worked hard to show appreciation for such a gift. The reality is that it has not always been easy. I have made numerous mistakes, celebrated many triumphs, and climbed out of multiple valleys. Actually, my story is probably no different from yours. On this journey called life, none of us are exempt from the many distractions that can get in the way of living the life God intended for us. **The lesson for me was learning these distractions are necessary pieces of our legacy, cleverly disguised as permanent disruptions. These distractions are merely life lessons that take the form of "temporary inconveniences" which bring opportunities to grow to the next best version of ourselves!"**

As I was having this discussion with one of my friends while preparing for an event, God placed the following words in my spirit **"ACTION ACTION... DESPITE THE DISTRACTION!!"** This has become my personal battle cry. Each time I share it from the stage, it resonates with the audience and I hope it does with you also. If I had quit when facing the various distractions of my life, we wouldn't be connected now.

The irony of my story is that I have faced every imaginable distraction in publishing this book for you, including loosing my final draft 2 weeks before the book release. I literally felt like I couldn't breathe. I shed a few tears, and then got out of my feelings and into **ACTION** to rebuild this manuscript. My Aunt Hyacinth cautioned that I may have shared my plans to publish this book way to soon, and probably with way too many people - which caused a series of delays. While that may in part be true (you can't always let the right hand know what the left hand is doing), I do know nothing happens before it's time. God needed me to experience a few more valuable lessons before sharing the complete story.

In this process, I have learned we cannot do this thing called life alone, and if we try to, we cause ourselves unnecessary headaches. However, we can continue to grow through life with the right support. It would be near impossible for me to measure the impact support has had in my life. It hurts my heart to hear from so many people I work with tell me they NEVER had anyone to support them in their goals and dreams. As I listened to their stories, it became clearer that part of my purpose is to be that support for others in taking **"ACTION ACTION... DESPITE THE DISTRACTION!!"**

PLEASE DON'T OVERCOMPLICATE THE ROAD TO WALKING IN OUR DESTINY BY FALLING PREY TO THE DISTRACTIONS IN OUR LIVES.

There will always be something to test our resolve and/or interrupt our progress. You just can't quit before your blessing. The ultimate purpose of this book is to transparently share 7 of the most challenging life lessons I have learned in order to walk in my destiny. Now as the old adage goes, "There is nothing new under the sun."; What is new, is our evolving paradigm shifts in how we appreciate the lessons learned. My prayer is this book joins the library of work that inspires you to THRIVE & LIVE your Divine Destiny Now!

The goal of each chapter is to create a sense of urgency around your goals and dreams! The 7 most prevalent distractions that challenge our ability to achieve our goals and live our dreams are lack of belief, procrastination, disorganization / lack of focus, toxic people, fear, ego, and selfishness.

When we move casually toward executing our divine assignment, we can create casualties if we miss the chance to save a life we were assigned to. I asked God to forgive me for anyone who may have stumbled because I didn't release this message sooner. Learn from my mistakes and move now with volume and velocity toward your goals and dreams… **"ACTION ACTION... DESPITE THE DISTRACTION!!"**

> *"The journey of a thousand miles begins with the first step."* Chinese Proverb

LET'S GET AQUAINTED

Before we get started, it is important for me to get to know **YOU**. You took the time to invest in this purchase and that means I want to take the time to learn about you and invest in your success. Please text the word DESTINY to 718-303-2966 so you can receive a free gift from me as a token of my appreciation. Thank you in advance. My desire is for this to be an experience we share and that requires two-way communication. Remember, we can't do this thing called life alone. I am invested in your success and excited about being a part of your journey during this time in your life!

RULES OF ENGAGEMENT

We all learn and process information differently. If you are the kind of person who likes to consume everything first and then go back and review the learning you can absolutely do that here. However, if you are willing to suspend the urge to go skip through all of the pages and just focus one chapter at a at a time, you will really get the value of a complete experience.

As I commit to you throughout your experience, I am asking you to commit to doing the following things daily while on this journey with anticipation that this will become part of your daily routine. After each chapter you can capture your **ACTION NOTES** in the space provided for you. Personalize this experience and make it your own.

1. **Prayer of Intention/Gratitude**
   As you read each lesson, I invite you to create the practice of saying a prayer of gratitude and intention. Starting from a place of gratitude allows you to focus on your blessings rather than your challenges. What you focus on expands so focus on expanding your blessings. Secondly, if we pray over our intentions we will manifest the specificity of our desires.

2. **Personal Lesson & Immediate Action**
   Capturing your thoughts, allows you to chronicle your journey and measure progress. As brilliant as we may be, we cannot remember everything. Getting in the habit of recording our thoughts allows your hand to be the digital recorder for your mind. You will be able to reflect on the lessons you learn, capture your thoughts and commit to an immediate ACTION as you review each lesson.

3. **Stretch Goals**
   I believe learning is reinforced by double ACTION. Usually the first time we hear, receive or see information it is on the surface. We need to repeat actions in order to truly absorb them. Challenge yourself to really stretch and grow during this portion of your journey. Someone very wise once said, "If you always do what you've always done, you will always get what you've always got." After each chapter you can create a stretch goal that will allow you to graduate to the next best version of yourself.

4. **Participation in Community**
   As I mentioned previously, we cannot do this thing called life alone. Working in community creates collective productivity. Knowing you are not alone helps to keep you inspired to continue taking action. If it is possible for one, it is possible for all. As my dear friends Che Brown & Trevor Otts would say, "Your take-away could be someone's big breakthrough!"

To this end, I invite you to join our private Destiny Designers® community on Facebook www.facebook.com/groups/DestinyDesignersU/ to continue the conversation. When you join, tag me in your posts so I can hear about your progress and we all can cheer you on. You can also follow & tag me on our other social media platforms:

Facebook:/DestinyDesignU

Twitter:@DestinyDesignU @StacieNCGrant

Instagram: @DestinyDesignU @StacieNCGrant

WHAT'S NOT IN MY BIO

"How can you step into the destiny God has for you if you don't feel worthy?" Oprah Winfrey

Giving myself permission to embrace my destiny was not an easy road. Many people look at who I am now without a clue of the road it took me to get here. I realized that there was an area in my life I needed to get past, so I could embrace the destiny God had in store for me. I had to overcome my own internal story, of whether or not I measured up or if I was enough. This was because I was comparing myself to the success of others and what or where I thought I should be. When I learned to really let go and let God, things started to shift. If we waste time trying to measure up to others we delay our innate ability to grow to the next best version of ourselves.

When I am speaking, training, hosting and facilitating… I am in perfect alignment with my DIVINE ASSIGNMENT! This is what makes my heart sing. I am often asked the question: "When did you first start speaking?" and I used to give my standard response of "it was during high school when I joined a leadership program", until I really sat still to think about where it all began. This was not easy because my mind was crowded with my most recent memories. Now, how far back can you remember the events of your childhood? I can clearly remember the excitement when I heard the ice cream truck come down our block, going to the local pool with my friends ,or when I would get my Friday treat of Pizza for only .25¢! I know I am dating myself…LOL. As for the others, I only recall them thanks to my mother's detailed account of these special memories.

Well, one such memory was my first day of school. I was dressed for the occasion and well adorned with bows and ribbons and my first book bag. My Mom took the day off because she anticipated that it would be a traumatic separation process for me. Much to her surprise it was quite the opposite. She pulled up to the school with my cousin and myself in the back seat. My cousin was very nervous and I was very anxious to get going. According to my mom's account of the story, I jumped out of the car, mounted my book bag, kissed her goodbye, spun on my heels and headed straight inside the school. Meanwhile, my cousin was crying and having a meltdown in the parking lot. Now my mom's day off was filled with calming my cousin down. When she returned to pick us up after school, the teacher asked to speak to her. Now you can imagine a certain level of concern when the teacher wants to talk to you on the first day of school. The teacher proceeded to share that she was impressed that I was able to read and seemed to be very bright. However, she had one challenge. "Stacie doesn't seem to acknowledge that I am the teacher because she keeps gathering all the children together to teach them their ABCs." So there you have it…I was destined to do this work. My purpose in life is to LEAD, TEACH, & INSPIRE! Higher levels bring bigger devils. I had numerous distractions along the way that tried to derail me but I could not be silenced and now I won't let anyone be silenced on my watch! *"ACTION ACTION... DESPITE THE DISTRACTION!!"*

You can probably relate if you can recall your earliest memories of what you were destined to do. You can find the hints about what you are destined to do by looking back at the things that have always come easy and natural to you. We tend to overlook our talents because they come easily to us. I don't know where your story begins, but you can choose now to be deliberate about the next chapter of your life and the results you seek. Remember these 7 Life Lessons are intended help you THRIVE and LIVE your DESTINY NOW! Let's do the work of moving forward together

"ACTION ACTION... DESPITE THE DISTRACTION!!" Let's get STARTED!!!

ORIENTATION

As an entrepreneur, one must be willing to make the nonnegotiable decision to continue taking **ACTION** until you reach your destination. You must be willing to use all that you have and all that you have been given to give birth to your goals and dreams. Initially when you set out to become an entrepreneur there is an excitement and thrill that runs through every cell in your body as you proudly declare to the world that you are in business for YOURSELF. When you realize you have a service or product that brings value to the marketplace, there is a certain sense of pride beaming from your face because after all, the world just became your oyster. Well what I know to be true is that there are going to be a series of tests that come your way as an entrepreneur. Some have described this as the universe testing how serious you are about what it is you want to bring to the marketplace. Others describe it as God's way of building your character and business muscle. What I know to be true is that being an entrepreneur is an ongoing learning process that will both test and strengthen your FAITH muscle.

Entrepreneurship is not for those who are weak at heart. It takes a special kind of person to set out on a road and a path of becoming an entrepreneur. Then add the notion that you may be in this world but not of the world. You have to find a way to move past the distractions that could take you out of alignment with God's will for your life. This book is about how to keep taking **ACTION** when these distractions happen. Most people shy away from embarking on the journey of entrepreneurship. They aren't willing to lose the comfort of a guaranteed paycheck and benefits to explore the unchartered territory and sometimes inconsistent income of an entrepreneur. So CONGRATULATIONS, you are a part of a select group of individuals willing to step out on FAITH and walk in their DIVINE DESTINY. We are clearly cut from the same cloth #Faithpreneurs. I just represent what is possible for your life.

On your journey, life will show up in interesting ways that will test your resolve to walk in your Divine Assignment. I had to find a way to encourage myself when there were no contracts, no money, limited to no support and a myriad of other obstacles. It was in answering a question at an event about how I was doing, that the following words leaped out of soul through my lips: **ACTION ACTION… DESPITE THE DISTRACTION!!** I was describing a challenge I was facing and that rose up in my spirit as the response. It became my battle cry and I invite you to make it yours. See when we are faced with challenges and opposition to our dreams, it's a battle to fight your way through. Warriors need a battle cry to motivate and keep them focused on defeating the enemy. When you start to second-guess your reasons to complete your divine assignment your battle cry will be **ACTION ACTION… DESPITE THE DISTRACTION!!** When everybody else seems to have given up and doesn't believe in your dream your battle cry will be: **ACTION ACTION… DESPITE THE DISTRACTION!!** When your goals and your dreams seem impossible to reach and all you have is that little voice and resolve inside telling you not to quit before you get your blessing. Let your battle cry continue to be **ACTION ACTION… DESPITE THE DISTRACTION!!**

My mission is to lead, teach, and inspire **Faithpreneurs** by interrupting the distractions that stop us from walking in our divine destiny and provide the platform to share our stories.

These life lessons are not meant to be a doctoral thesis, rather they are insights into the lessons that have impacted my life and allowed me to walk in my DESTINY and may do the same for you!!!

DISTRACTION
ALERT

Lack of belief

Lack of belief haunts the best of us. We tend to question our value, abilities, and capacity to live our best life. We wonder things like: Can I do this? Am I worthy? Is this the right time? Will it work? Do I deserve to win? Will I be successful? The truth is we will never know the answers to these questions unless we step out on FAITH! Our beliefs show up in our behavior. We run away from our divine assignment if we don't believe we are equipped to accomplish it. Author Mark Batterson said it best, "God doesn't call the qualified, he qualifies the called." Simply put, if we walk in the FAITH of unlimited possibilities we won't have time to linger in the shadow of disbelief.

LIFE LESSON 1

FAITH IS AN ACTION WORD!

For me there is no "separation of church and state". I am clear that this platform is a blessing and one I wouldn't have without God's grace and mercy over my life. Early on in my speaking career I was warned not to talk about my faith to audiences as it may alienate or offend some people. Instead I was urged to use more general terms and references that would vaguely reference my FAITH. It is unfortunate that throughout history, many have used religion to wage war and justify the unjust treatment of others for their selfish intentions but the God I serve will have a just reward for those who have misrepresented His truth. My intent never has been and never will be to offend anyone but I won't deny my God. I will however boldly proclaim my FAITH. Without God I would not be able to share these words with you and see the impact they have in the lives of those I have been able to serve.

My earliest memories as a child include going to church with my Grandmother faithfully every week and attending Sunday School. It was there I learned fun songs and rhymes to help me memorize all the books of the Bible, some of which I still use today to quickly look up scriptures. At that stage in my life, my FAITH consisted of knowing that God loved everyone, especially little children.

Then when I was about 8 years old, my mother started attending church on a regular basis. This was after taking a few years off from church attendance after migrating to the United States from Jamaica where as a child church was mandatory every week. Something was different this time when she met the late Rev. Mother Cora Paris. Under this ministry, she began to develop a personal relationship with God for herself. She no longer went to church on holidays or special occasions. She had a zeal and commitment to grow deeper in the word of God. I witnessed the change in my mother at this early age and I too started attending church regularly with her.

As I grew older, I enjoyed my time in church and the social relationships with my friends who became family to me. Church was just a part of the natural ebb and flow of my life. I attended not just because it was compulsory but because I also enjoyed the fellowship and learning about the love of God. The tail end of my teenage years started to present a few distractions, like parties, social activities and boys. There were numerous weekends I spent "turning up" on Saturday and arriving to church on Sunday morning fighting to keep my eyes open.

A few years passed as I juggled my dual lifestyle until one day my pastor said to me, "You should be bringing your friends with you to church instead of them pulling you out. You can't serve two masters." Those words hit me deep down in my soul. Initially I felt good I was at least coming to church but I couldn't keep juggling both. It took me a little while longer to really understand the magnitude of my decisions. It wasn't that I couldn't go out or have a social life, but I couldn't let that consume my heart's desire and distract me from developing my personal relationship with God and strengthen my FAITH.

When I made the decision to spend a little more time working on my spiritual growth (putting my faith in action) my desire to hang out all the time organically started to diminish. I still enjoyed hanging out with friends but I wasn't consumed with planning for the next party or club experience. I became more and more interested in understanding my personal relationship with God. Contrary to public opinion, God is not a big intimidating ogre standing with an

14

ax of damnation over your head. Rather, He is a loving, peaceful Lord waiting with open arms to receive all who choose to exercise their free will to serve Him in spirit and truth.

By now, if you are not a Christian you may feel as if I am trying to convert you but that is not my primary goal, albeit it would be an awesome byproduct. My goal is to share how growing deeper in my FAITH has given me the strength to take **ACTION ACTION... DESPITE THE DISTRACTION** through the valleys of life.

If you were to research the meaning of the word FAITH you would find it defined as a belief in the existence of God, something that is believed with strong conviction or a firm belief in something of which there is no proof. In all these definitions, the common word is BELIEF. We all consciously or unconsciously believe in something, your beliefs show up in your behavior. If you believe that there is no God to have FAITH in, you believe you can do whatever you desire with no eternal consequences. If you, like me, believe there is a God you choose to live a life powered by FAITH and obedience to God's word.

The lesson I learned is FAITH is an **ACTION** word only when you exercise it. Living a life of FAITH requires you to draw from your beliefs in every area of your life. It is easy to boast of FAITH when things in our life are doing well but what do we do when the challenges of life show up at our door? This is when we have to put our beliefs into **ACTION**. The sum of these actions then creates the positive changes we seek in our lives.

Choosing the narrow vs. the wide road is a constant challenge for those who choose to serve God. The world presents many enticing distractions that can entice us to adopt behavior that doesn't honor our FAITH. We can get caught up with pursuing fame and fortune by any means necessary instead of being mastered by the word of God, which will enable us to be in alignment with our destiny. This doesn't mean that you can't be blessed with wealth and great fortune. What it means is that we truly believe FAITH is an **ACTION** word, we put God first and ask Him to direct our path. What He has for you is for you and no one and nothing can change that. It took me a while to really understand the power in that truth. I didn't have to chase after what I saw other people doing or take an unethical path to fulfill my destiny. No, I just had to walk boldly in it by being obedient to what my FAITH has taught me.

Through exercising my FAITH I founded Destiny Designers University ®, a virtual training platform that allows us to graduate to the best next version of ourselves by turning inspiration into results. I wasn't sure about the original structure of Destiny Designers University and started to become overwhelmed with suggestions from my well-meaning friends. I started to feel stressed and anxious and those two emotions are not our friends. I had to block out everyone else's voice in order to hear God. Sometimes you have to sit still so you can listen and be in alignment with your assignment. I didn't know what the outcome would be but I started to put my FAITH in action and asking God to direct my path. All I can say is God can surely dream a bigger dream for you than you could ever dream for yourself.

Only you know what has been placed on your heart, what is bubbling up in your spirit, what you know you have been put on the planet to do. Taking action on those dreams requires an unwavering FAITH in knowing that if God gave it to you, He will also make the provision for you to manifest it. Dr. Martin Luther King, Jr. said it best, *"Faith is taking the first step even if you don't see the entire staircase."* My journey has been and continues to be a process. I had to make a decision to walk by FAITH and not by sight. Just because I couldn't see how the bills would be paid, how the contract would be signed or how the healing and restoration would happen, I had to take daily action to exercise my FAITH that God's word will never return unto Him void. No matter what situations look like, it is building up our FAITH that removes doubt about getting through every trial, challenge or obstacle.

What we need is a reference point that can remind us of a time in our lives when what we wanted seemed impossible, manifested in front of our very own eyes. For me, it was after years of planning events for my clients, that I had a desire to host my own. Even after the prompting of my colleagues, clients and friends, I was hesitant because I didn't have the budget, or resources for such an undertaking, but I prayed to God for guidance and direction because NOTHING works until YOU do. Scripture tells me, that *"For as the body without the spirit is dead, so faith without works is dead also."* James 2:26 KJV

Well, I started researching venues and found the perfect space. I still didn't have the budget but by putting my FAITH in ACTION, I was able to negotiate a payment plan with the venue that would allow me to sell tickets to the event and generate the budget we needed. It was nerve racking signing that contract but I was truly walking by FAITH. Gratefully, I had a supportive husband whose FAITH was as strong as mine and a husband who believed in & supported my vision. After the venue was secured, we created the event promotion and began selling tickets. I can still remember staring at the computer waiting for the first sale as if my eyes could magically make them come in faster …LOL.

Registrations started to increase and I can't even explain how I connected with angel investors, how partnerships were created and how resources became available except as a reward for putting my FAITH in **ACTION**. Dreams are beautiful but they only become meaningful when they become REALITY and that takes **ACTION!** My first Create Your Own Luck Seminar was a huge success. Here is a copy of the flyer.

I was so excited about the outcome and the testimonies we received from the event. I was even more grateful for my friends who agreed to be presenters. In chapter 4, I will be discussing the lessons I have learned concerning relationships but I have to pause here and publicly thank 5 of my dear friends for having my back for this event; Andrew Morrison, Jay Brunson, John Crant, Cathleen Williams, Esq. & Lucinda Cross. I love them to the moon and back for ALWAYS being willing to be a blessing in my life.

Well I went on to host 2 additional Create Your Own Luck Seminars. Special thanks to Dominique Reese, Tiffany "The Budgetnista" Aliche, Shareeke Edmead-Nesi, Stacie L. Price, Ajshay James and Dr. Robert Scott for their support.

Now, I am sure you are expecting me to tell you that I continued these seminars and yielded large profits from them over the last 5 years. Well, I didn't for one reason and one reason only; I didn't continue taking **ACTION** on my goals and dreams. Instead I created a new default position. I put my energy and resources into building other people's dreams and platforms. Now, there is nothing wrong with this, as I have always been a servant leader but we have to be careful not to get comfortable with staying in a support role when we are meant to lead. Even though God showed me what He could do, I doubted my ability to sustain my growth and expansion. Honestly, it was easier to lend my talent and expertise to other brands vs. being diligent about expanding my own platform.

It took a while for me to own my truth but I don't regret what I was able to learn in the process. All I had to do was put my FAITH in **ACTION** once again and move forward with expanding my platform; hence the birth of Destiny Designers University ® November 29, 2014. Building out this platform not only allows me to continue my live events but continue to put my FAITH in **ACTION** as we endeavor to create a full multi-media personal growth and development corporation.

#FaithpreneurFootnote:

> *"Now faith is the substance of things hoped for, the evidence of things not seen. But without faith it is impossible to please him; for he that cometh to God must believe that he is and that he is a rewarder of them that diligently seek him."* Hebrews 11:1 & 6 KJV

God gives us the free will to choose to serve Him in spirit and truth. If we choose to serve Him, we can't have a dual confession. Either we believe He can do ALL not just some things. Either we believe that if we ask for His direction, He will order our steps. When we are building our businesses we will have to exercise our FAITH that if God gave us the vision, He will make the provision.

> *"Write the vision and make it plain upon tables, that he may run that readeth it. For the vision is yet for an appointed time, but at the end it shall speak, and not lie: though it tarry, wait for it; because it will surely come, it will not tarry."*
> Habakkuk 2:2-3 KJV

When we confess our FAITH others are watching us to see how we stand even in the midst of the storms in our life. Writing our vision is just one part of the equation. The most important part is asking God for direction so we can be in alignment with His will for our lives. I didn't always get this right. I always learned about the importance of setting goals so that is what I started doing. The challenge was that I was making my goals and telling God to bless them rather than asking Him what His will was for my life so my life would be blessed. Once I learned to decrease so that God's will could be done in my life, I received my increase. My vision was now focused on being in alignment with the assignment God had already placed on my life.

Take the time to sit still and listen to God's voice. Don't be like me and overcomplicate your journey. God doesn't intend for us to struggle unnecessarily. He is always patiently waiting for us to be obedient so He can do His best work through us. Be mindful of the distractions that tempt you to listen to other people's voices instead of that of the Holy Spirit. Not everything is for everybody.

Sometimes the vision of the future still makes my heart skip a few beats but nothing compares to walking in my Divine Assignment. When you think about your goals and dreams, are you satisfied with your pursuit of them? Are you boldly moving forward in FAITH and taking consistent ACTION or are you making excuses about the right time and overthinking taking the next step?

When you start to second-guess your divine assignment remember our battle cry **"ACTION ACTION… DESPITE THE DISTRACTION!!"** When you feel overwhelmed with the opinions of others, remember to silence them, sit still so you can hear God's voice and take **"ACTION ACTION… DESPITE THE DISTRACTION!!"**

Take a few moments to capture your
"#ACTIONNOTES" below:

MY PRAYER OF GRATITUDE & INTENTION...:

_____

_____

_____

_____

_____

THE LESSON FOR ME IS...:

_____

_____

_____

_____

_____

_____

MY IMMEDIATE ACTION DESPITE THE DISTRACTION OF LACK OF BELIEF WILL BE TO:

_____

_____

_____

_____

_____

_____

MY STRETCH GOAL...

_____

_____

_____

_____

_____

_____

Remember to share your takeaways with us at:
Facebook:/DestinyDesignU

Twitter:@DestinyDesignU @StacieNCGrant

Instagram: @DestinyDesignU @StacieNCGrant

DISTRACTION
ALERT

Procrastination

If you have ever been caught in the valley of procrastination, please raise your hand. Trust and know that my hand was up as well. Procrastination is one of the most popular distractions the majority of us face. It is an easy default position to let our self off the hook when we don't feel like getting a task done. If we put things off one time, it can easily go from occasionally to routinely putting off for later what we can do NOW.

LIFE LESSON 2

"IT'S NOT ABOUT BEING PERFECT; IT'S ABOUT GETTING STARTED IN ORDER TO HAVE SOMETHING TO PERFECT."

When is it ever the perfect time to do anything? Don't be paralyzed by the pursuit of perfection, rather be consumed with the process of completion. How can you perfect something if you haven't started anything? If I had waited for Destiny Designers University® to be perfect, you wouldn't be reading this book today.

Even one of the biggest brands in the world releases a new phone at least once a year. Inevitably the phone has numerous bugs that get fixed after the release. You guessed it. I am talking about Apple. They don't wait for their IPhones to be perfect on each new release, they perfect it along the way. Success leaves clues.

How many things have you delayed in your life waiting on the perfect time, perfect financing, perfect relationships, perfect resources, etc. Once you start moving forward, you will be surprised on how providence will step in and pave the road to perfection.

We have to move with the urgency of now towards our goals and dreams! It's now or never… your dreams can't wait." These past few years I feel like I have attended one too many funerals. Each one reminding me that life is a gift and time is not guaranteed. Rev. Myles Munroe referred to the graveyard as the richest place on earth because that were so many dreams unfulfilled that lay buried beneath the earth.

Getting started is not easy but it is possible if you have a plan. Your plan can't just be a long to-do list because that will cause even more anxiety, which will ultimately lead to inaction. The reality is all of us juggle multiple things each day. The challenge is getting to the end of our to-do list. That's why I developed a process in my Destiny Designers University® that we call the **DAILY FOCUS OF 3** to start taking **ACTION**.

The first step of the **DAILY FOCUS OF 3** is to choose what time of day works best for you to plan; early mornings before you start your day or late night before you go to sleep. Next, decide what the three most important items are you need to accomplish for the day. There will always be more than 3 things to do in any given day but what this technique does is build momentum in your productivity. You will feel a sense of accomplishment when you have a completed list for the day. For this process to work you have to resist the temptation of adding more than 3 things to the list. Once those three things are completed feel free to work on other things. The irony is that by focusing just on completing your 3 items, you gain more momentum to get additional tasks completed. You can guarantee that if you stay focused you can get at least 21 items completed in one week, 84 more in a month and over 1000 in a year.

Try utilizing the following **DAILY FOCUS OF 3 WEEKLY ACTION PLAN** below. Get started **NOW!** Don't fill it out all at once. Come back and fill in the information daily. Put a bookmark in this page & focus on just 3 items per day. Cross off all completed tasks before you plan for the next day.

Day 1

1. _____

2. _____

3. _____

Day 2

1. _____
2. _____
3. _____

Day 3

1. _____
2. _____
3. _____

Day 4

1. _____
2. _____
3. _____

Day 5

1. _____
2. _____
3. _____

Day 6

1. _____
2. _____
3. _____

Day 7

1. _____
2. _____
3. _____

CONGRATULATIONS!!! You are no longer in the valley of procrastination. You are on the mountaintop of completion. You have completed a minimum of 21 items this week that you are perfecting along the way. If you continue, imagine just how productive the next chapter of your life will be.

#EntrepreneurSidebar

BUSY VS. PRODUCTIVE

I can't tally how many hours I have spent busy with meetings, phone calls or other activities that weren't productive. Busy doesn't guarantee that you are being productive. It just gives the appearance that you are. As entrepreneurs, our income depends on income producing activities. It is very easy to get caught up in busy work vs. productivity. Sales = Productivity. As you focus on your **DAILY FOCUS OF 3** make sure at least one item is an income producing activity.

#FaithpreneurFootnote:

"In all thy ways acknowledge him, and he shall direct thy paths." Proverbs 3:6 KJV

When we put God first we receive the clarity we need in our daily activities. As we continue to press toward the mark, we can approach each day with the confidence that our steps have already been ordered.

" And we know all things work together for good to them that love God, to them who are the called according to his purpose." Romans 8:28 KJV

Nothing we grow through is wasted. Each experience is a part of our journey. We are all either just coming out of something, in the middle of something or about to experience something. No matter how life shows up, our FAITH reminds us that ALL things will work together for good.

When you start to feel like you are falling back into the valley of procrastination remember our battle cry **"ACTION ACTION... DESPITE THE DISTRACTION!!"** and just GET STARTED!!!

> ## Take a few moments to capture your "#ACTIONNOTES" below:

MY PRAYER OF GRATITUDE & INTENTION...:

_____

_____

_____

_____

_____

_____

THE LESSON FOR ME IS...:

_____

_____

_____

_____

_____

_____

MY IMMEDIATE ACTION DESPITE THE DISTRACTION OF PROCRASTINATION WILL BE TO:

_____

_____

_____

_____

_____

_____

MY STRETCH GOAL...

_____

_____

_____

_____

_____

Remember to share your takeaways with us at:
Facebook:/DestinyDesignU

Twitter:@DestinyDesignU @StacieNCGrant

Instagram: @DestinyDesignU @StacieNCGrant

DISTRACTION
ALERT

Disorganization/lack of focus

The temptation is to act on every idea we have all at the same time and that would make us insane. There is no crime in having great ideas & plans. The danger is when we don't develop an organized plan to execute them or the focus to see them through. Without a clear end goal, we waste one of the most precious commodities we have, TIME! When we have established a goal it will require more than the minimum disciplined effort to achieve maximum results.

LIFE LESSON 3

DISCIPLINE REQUIRES MORE THAN THE MINIMUM!

Discipline sounds good in theory but the ability to develop discipline in every area of our lives can be quite challenging. From remembering our earliest lessons with personal grooming, to doing our homework every night, or taking our vitamins everyday – all these tasks required discipline. If we did them well, it required more than minimum effort. It required an additional, consistent resolve to master any given task. Those who excel at anything in life are usually those who exercise more than the minimum discipline to see their goal through. There is no escaping the amount of work necessary to reap the rewards of discipline in our life. Let's use school for an example. Without discipline you could, as my Father would say, "graduate with attendance" or with discipline they could graduate as Valedictorian. The truth is NOTHING works unless YOU do! We get in life what we work for, not what we wish for. Minimal effort yields minimal results.

When I think of the people I admire, they took the time to discipline themselves in mastering their craft. World famous athlete Michael Jordan had the discipline to rise early every morning to practice hours before his teammates. His legacy as "Air Jordan" didn't just fall out of the sky. He had to develop the discipline to maintain a more than the minimum work ethic. It couldn't have been easy for him to sacrifice sleep to rise early every day to condition his body to win. It takes a certain kind of resolve to develop this kind of discipline. In the pursuit of our dreams we reach a point where we have to decide if we are comfortable with average or willing to do more than the minimum to be extraordinary! I am sure Michael Jordon didn't know what his legacy would be while he was practicing every morning. He was solely focused on mastering the game. He put in what Malcolm Gladwell refers to as 10K hours of mastery in his book "The Outliers". Michael Jordan kept his focus on stretching beyond what was comfortable and/or easy and demanded excellence in every performance.

Where can we do more than minimum to create new disciplines for success in our own lives? I meet people in many of the audiences I speak in front of who can quote, post and/or re-tweet every motivational phrase in the personal growth and development space but haven't exercised the discipline to produce results in their own lives.

This is what inspired my creation of Destiny Designers University® as a personal growth and development platform for #Faithpreneurs that seeks to create synergy in the spiritual, mental, physical and financial areas of our lives. We learn and grow in collaborative achievement driven community by turning inspiration into RESULTS! In order to get to these results we have to exercise the discipline to do more than minimum.

What does more than minimum look like in our SPIRITUAL life?

The word spiritual life may have different connotations for some people. For me, spiritual life means a belief in and commitment to God as the head of my life. In order to maintain focused discipline in our spiritual life we have to make a commitment to be mastered by the word of God. This means we have to read more than the 23rd Psalm and attend Church more than one Sunday a month or just on holidays. We weren't created to do this thing called life alone. That's why God places us in communities of FAITH to fellowship and grow together. When we give God His time he rewards our obedience and sacrifice. When we grow in his word we get stronger in our FAITH and we are able to stand through the storms of life knowing that God has already worked it out.

We have to deliberately carve out time to pray daily and read our Bible. If not the day will fly by and we rush in a prayer or barely crack open our Bible before sleep consumes us. More than minimum efforts requires us to truly put God first not just in words but in action. People often ask me how I remain so positive even when I am going through the most challenging times. My answer is how can I say I have FAITH and that God is control of my life and then worry in the next breath. The two don't go together. I acknowledge the trial or tribulation for what it is, seek to learn the lesson or recognize the attack and then choose to believe and trust my God will handle it.

What does more than minimum look like in our MENTAL life?

If what we focus on expands, we must be selective of what we allow in our consciousness. We can't allow anyone or anything to sow seeds of discord in the fields of our peace. We must work on maintaining a positive and healthy mindset. Such peace is not just going to happen. We have to do more than the minimum to pull out the weeds of discord as they try to take root in our minds. If we allow the wrong thoughts to fester and grow for one minute too long, we can slip into dangerous areas of misery and depression. We must develop a disciplined mental regime that will fortify our thoughts. Here are three ways you can strengthen your mental discipline:

1. **READ 15-30 MINUTES OF NON-FICTION DAILY**
   We are all works in progress. We don't reach a magical age where we know everything. Once there's breath, there is hope and once there is hope there is opportunity to grow and learn. Some of my mentors are over 70 years old and they still invest in their personal growth and development by reading

a new book every month, attending conferences and even navigating social media. Once our brain expands it can no longer return to its original form. If you are a life long student you have probably amassed tons of books and magazines over the years. Brush off the dust off one and just read 15 min a day until you make a dent in your personal library.

2. **PRACTICE FORGIVENESS**
Unfortunately we are not exempt from experiencing hurt, disappointment and betrayal in our lives. When we feel pain our instinct is to hold on to these emotions, churning them over and over again in our minds, maybe even plotting revenge. The pain is real and letting go of this kind of toxic energy is not easy. What we don't realize is that every moment we hold on to these emotions it eats away at the fabric of our soul. In practicing forgiveness, learn to forgive yourself first and extend the same courtesy to others even if it appears they don't deserve to be forgiven. Practicing forgiveness frees your spirit and allows more room for happiness to fill your soul.

3. **SHARE LOVE AND EXPRESS GRATITUDE**
My typical greeting is "Hello Sunshine". I love to see the smile on people's faces when they receive the love in my greeting. People often ask me why I am always so positive. I just love to share love and receive love. That is why I limit my interaction with miserable people. It is a choice to be positive, even on the most challenging of days. When I am experiencing difficulty feeling positive, I shift my energy to a place of gratitude just for life. That is usually the self-correction I need to not waste a moment entertaining anything but love in me and around me. Gratitude allows you to shift your perspective and find the love in the details. Some people keep gratitude journals to remind themselves of the smallest of blessings. I make it apart of my daily meditation. Choose to share love and find gratitude in every moment of your life.

What does more than minimum look like in our PHYSICAL life?

We only get one body and if we don't take care of our temple, we won't be alive to enjoy the fruits of our labor. Let me confess that I struggle daily with focused discipline in my physical life. I would much rather watch other people work out and the weight fall off of me. Unfortunately there is no short cut to proper nutrition and regular exercise. Take it from a recovering "foodie", we do have the capacity to do more than the minimum in our physical life if we make ourselves a priority. The key is not trying to do it alone if you can find an accountability partner or community that can support you in the process. Working in community keeps you focused especially on the days you feel weak. I lost the most weight in a 90-day health challenge where I was accountable to a group. What this proved to me was that if I was willing to do more than the minimum, I could discipline my self to maintain a healthy lifestyle. As my mentor Les Brown said to me "Nothing tastes as good as healthy feels." We are all works in progress so even if we slip, we can just pick back up and focus on the healthy habits and the unhealthy habits will fall off. A healthy lifestyle is a profit not a punishment. Just continue to pray for me as I am still in snicker bar and chicken wing rehab …LOL.

What does more than minimum look like in our FINANCIAL life?

Shopping has got to be one of the most exciting pastimes of all time. The only challenge is that excitement is usually quickly tainted by buyer's remorse. My Dad tried to warn me as a teenager that if you didn't have the cash to purchase something that meant you couldn't afford it. Well I seemed to have forgotten that golden nugget when I received a slew of credit card applications in my freshman year of college. I was so excited about the idea of having my very own credit card, complete with my middle initial. You couldn't tell me anything! I was finally grown and in charge of my own destiny. What I didn't realize was this new found independence was going to lure me into a dangerous false sense of financial control. I started off pretty good not charging too much and paying my bills on time. After my Freshman year, I thought I was on a role but somewhere along the line, I started increasing my purchases because I had the money on my credit limit. This was the beginning of a slippery slope of unwise spending habits. Credit cards seemed to be the perfect way to get what I needed if I didn't have to cash handy since I had time to get at least the minimum payment together.

Fast forward to adult life. You can get caught up working just to pay the bills we create on credit. It starts with one card and can easily mushroom into over 5 credit cards you are juggling to manage; everything from 2 of the 3 major credit cards to one from each of your favorite stores. As long as we can juggle payment cycles and not totally exceed the spending limits, we feel we are doing well. The truth is this can become quite exhausting and emotionally draining. At a certain point you can start to feel hopeless and depressed about the prospects of ever becoming debt free. This is a common story for many people but how the story ends depends on being willing to change our financial behavior.

Financial Advisor I am not, but I do know a few behaviors that can increase your ability to live debt free. Now let me also note that credit cards are an excellent way to leverage buying power. The key is the discipline to manage your spending in order not to get in debt. Here are a few recommendations:

1. Consult/Hire a Financial Advisor
2. Make a Budget
3. Save 10% of your income
4. Pay off the credit cards with the highest interest rates first
5. Live below your means

#FaithpreneurFootnote:

"And be not conformed to this world: but be ye transformed by the renewing of your mind, that ye may prove what is that good, and acceptable, and perfect will of God." Romans 12:2 KJV

As we seek to be in alignment with God's will for our life, we have to remember that our process may be in direct conflict with the ways of the world. While we are all God's creation, we are all not His people. Simply put, if one doesn't believe that God is an authority over one's life, then that individual will not be governed by or obedient to what God's word instructs us to do. To this end, I am grateful to my spiritual Mom, for sharing this prayer with our congregation.

A PRAYER FOR SPIRITUAL GROWTH

Lord, give me the discipline I need to cultivate a life of consistent growth in you. Grant me the discernment to see the subtlety of satan as he works to oppress my life. Give me a teachable spirit so I can receive correction and instruction from you. Eliminate the spiritual weeds that hinder my growth. Make my enemies my footstool, and deliver me from all evil. AMEN

Rev. Mother Cora Paris

When you start to feel disorganized or you are lacking focus remember our battle cry **"ACTION ACTION… DESPITE THE DISTRACTION!!"** Start wherever you are with whatever you have to begin to incorporate the focused discipline you need to do more than the minimum for your goals and dreams.

Take a few moments to capture your
"#ACTIONNOTES" below:

MY PRAYER OF GRATITUDE & INTENTION...:

_____

_____

_____

_____

_____

_____

THE LESSON FOR ME IS...:

_____

_____

_____

_____

_____

_____

MY IMMEDIATE ACTION DESPITE THE DISTRACTION OF
DISORGANIZATION/ LACK OF FOCUS WILL BE TO:

_____

_____

_____

_____

_____

_____

MY STRETCH GOAL...

_____

_____

_____

_____

_____

_____

Remember to share your takeaways with us at:
Facebook:/DestinyDesignU

Twitter:@DestinyDesignU @StacieNCGrant

Instagram: @DestinyDesignU @StacieNCGrant

DISTRACTION
ALERT

Toxic people

Toxic people will literally drain the life out of you if you let them. I identify toxic people as individuals who constantly complain, love drama, create conflict lie, cheat, betray your trust, etc. These individuals always see the glass half empty instead of half full. Sometimes it's hard escaping these individuals, especially if they are in your family but what you can do is limit your interaction with them. Toxic energy is a cancer that attacks your spirit. The treatment is complete removal or limited interaction with toxic people.

LIFE LESSON 4

NEVER SUBSTITUTE QUANTITY FOR QUALITY IN YOUR FRONT ROW!

Everyone wants to feel loved or at the very least appreciated. We will go to great lengths to elicit these emotions from others. In this age of social media, many people feel validated by the amount of friends or likes they have. It is a false sense of achievement. It is not the quantity of relationships that validate us; it is the quality of these relationships that support us on our journey. It is the joy in knowing that you have unconditional love from people who truly know you. It is the comfort in knowing that you are not being judged but rather supported and when you do receive constructive criticism it is coming from a place of love.

I wasn't always clear about the importance of quality relationships in my life. Even as a child I always love interacting with people so I always had what I thought were many friends. My mother used to often caution me about referring to everyone as friends. She said that not everybody's your friend most of them are just acquaintances. I just couldn't believe that to be true. Why wouldn't everyone that I love & support not love & support me the same way?

It seems so simple, but unfortunately I would learn just how complicated the answer to this question was.

We have to train people on how to treat us by being clear about our expectations. We can't expect people to show up in our lives the way we would like without clearly articulating to them what we desire. Just as we should be willing to ask those that we care about how we can support them in the way in which they desire. Communication is key in building quality relationships and the only way we can effectively sustain them. I train on the topic of feedback, which allows you to understand, process and to engage in effective communication. What I have come to realize is if we could take the extra time to communicate with clarity, there would be a whole lot more peace in the world.

The love is truly in the details. With my schedule, it is hard to communicate with everyone as often as I would like. To compensate for this, I always make a personal phone call to those that I'm close to for their birthday. This may not seem like a major undertaking but trust me when I tell you that they wait for their annual birthday song and if I don't call early enough they have a slight attitude. It reminds them that I have them in my heart even if we don't get to communicate everyday. Put the love in the details of your relationships and pay it forward. Your reward will be greater.

Over the years I have shared a passage I found years ago that captured my feelings about the quality of people in your life. It had no title and no author so I named it **FRONT ROW**.

FRONT ROW

Invite your audience carefully.
Not everyone is healthy enough to
have a front row seat in our lives.
There are some people in your
life that need to be loved from a distance.

It's amazing what you can
accomplish when you let go, or at least minimize your time
with draining, negative, incompatible,
not-going-anywhere relationships/friendships.

Observe the relationships around you.
Pay attention.
Which ones lift and which ones lean?
Which one encourage and
which ones discourage?
Which ones are on a path of growth uphill and which
ones are going downhill?
When you leave certain people, do you feel better or feel worse?
Which ones always have drama or don't really understand,
know or appreciate you?

The more you seek quality, respect, growth, peace of mind, love
and truth around you, the easier it will become for you to decide
who gets to sit in the FRONT ROW and who should be moved to
the balcony of your life!

You cannot change the people around you...
but you can change the people you are around!

Author Unknown

This is a loaded passage. The first time I read it my mouth dropped
as I recognized some of the people it described in my own life. It's
hard acknowledging the truth about your relationships, especially
when they are people you love. Sometimes, you have to love them
from a distance & let your example encourage them on their own
path of personal growth.

As an entrepreneur, you no longer have the luxury to associate with
just anyone. Casual associations can cause casualties. We have to be
very deliberate on who we spend our time with – who we allow to
peer into our dream.

Everyone that came with you may not be able to stay with you if
they are on your same journey of consistent personal growth and
development. As you elevate your consciousness it is very difficult to

remain in conversation with those who refuse to grow. When others accuse you of changing, don't get defensive. Just agree because you have changed for the better and prayerfully your example will encourage them to do the same.

I am so blessed to have the support of my family and friends who believe in my dream. Even though along the way I know a few of them would say, "Stacie has been at this for a long time, I sure hope it works." In the very next breath they would ask me what they could do to help. People in your **FRONT ROW** anticipate your needs while those who need to be moved to the balcony of your life, only ask for what they need from you.

Who is sitting in your **FRONT ROW**? As you evaluate your relationships, are you satisfied or do you need to make some adjustments? Here are a few questions to assist you in your evaluation: Does the thought of them bring a smile to your face? Are your conversations one-sided or reciprocal? or Do they inspire you to grow? As you answer these and other questions, about who is sitting in your **FRONT ROW**, take inventory of how you show up in the **FRONT ROW** of those you love.

#EntrepreneurSidebar

GIVE THE BENEFIT OF THE DOUBT

One of my pet peeves is listening to people make assumptions without getting clarification. Resist the temptation to pass judgment rather than giving someone the benefit of the doubt. All of us are works in progress so you should associate with people who are as committed to their own personal growth and development as you are. Sometimes all it takes is one conversation to bring clarity. As we grow through life, the quality of our relationships are PRICELESS and worth the investment of our time to sustain them!

#FaithpreneurFootnote:

> *"Finally, brethren, whatsoever things are honest, whatsoever things are just, whatsoever things are pure, whatsoever things are lovely, whatsoever things are of a good report; if there be any virtue, and if there be any praise think on these things."* Ephesians 4:8 KJV

God's word gives us the perfect roadmap to live our lives. The difficulty is staying headed to His instructions. He didn't intend for us to journey through life alone, thus He places us in fellowship with one another. An old wise tale states "Show me your friends, show me who you are." It is so important that the people who sit in your **FRONT ROW** share your common beliefs. If you make it a habit to think on the right things individually you can create AMAZING things together! It has been the people in my **FRONT ROW** that has helped me weather the storms of life, celebrate the victories and share the lessons. During each step of the process our vision becomes clearer.

When you identify that toxic people have invaded your space remember our battle cry **"ACTION ACTION… DESPITE THE DISTRACTION!!"** as you remove them and/or move them to the balcony of your life.

Take a few moments to capture your
"#ACTIONNOTES" below:

MY PRAYER OF GRATITUDE & INTENTION...:

_____

_____

_____

_____

_____

_____

THE LESSON FOR ME IS...:

_____

_____

_____

_____

_____

_____

**MY IMMEDIATE ACTION DESPITE THE DISTRACTION OF
TOXIC PEOPLE WILL BE TO:**

_____

_____

_____

_____

_____

_____

MY STRETCH GOAL...

_____

_____

_____

_____

_____

_____

Remember to share your takeaways with us at:
Facebook:/DestinyDesignU

Twitter:@DestinyDesignU @StacieNCGrant

Instagram: @DestinyDesignU @StacieNCGrant

DISTRACTION
ALERT

Fear

President Franklin D. Roosevelt is quoted as saying "The only thing we have to fear is fear itself." While this is true, I think W. Clement Stone said it best "Thinking will not overcome fear but **ACTION** will." There is no getting away from the anxious feeling when approaching a new task, moment or opportunity. What we can do is face our fears by taking the first nervous step and by the third & fourth step you will begin to find your own rhythm. This is when you will realize what a minor distraction fear really is.

LIFE LESSON 5

CREATE YOUR OWN LUCK; LUCK DOESN'T JUST HAPPEN... YOU HAVE TO CREATE IT!!

The base of my platform is in tribute to my Grandmother Pernell "Pearl" Agatha Rhoden. She received her angel wings December 15, 2015 and there is not a day that goes by that my family and I don't miss her physical presence. We find peace in knowing her spirit will never leave us and we honor her legacy in how we live our life. My first product was a tribute to the first lesson I received about the concept of luck.

Growing up there always seemed to be a saying that my Jamaican grandparents would have to share. Each of these sayings were typically loaded with life lessons that all of us grandchildren didn't appreciate until we got older. There was one however, that resonated with me that I heard over and over again.

The first time I heard it, was coming home excited about the prospect of being in the school play. I was very fortunate that I grew up in a three family home where my grandparents lived on the second floor so I had their care after school when my Mother was working. This particular day I remember rushing home to tell my grandmother the story about the school play. How I really wanted to audition for the lead role in the play but I didn't think I was going to get picked. I told her I wasn't the smartest or cutest girl in the class, so I wouldn't be lucky enough to get chosen.

Well, I remember my grandmother put her hand on hip, turned to me and said in her Jamaican accent "Luck… luck na ave noting to do wid it !!! **COURAGE AND WILL PERSEVERANCE AND SKILL THESE ARE THE FOUR LEAVES OF LUCK'S CLOVER!"** At that age I had no clue about what a clover was, much less a four-leaf clover. I still didn't know what that had to do with me getting the role in the play...LOL. It took me a few years to grasp the magnitude of that lesson and the impact it would have in helping the masses create their own luck!

COURAGE is the leaf that holds the strength to face the challenges in your life and move forward anyway. Entrepreneurs create the solutions for the world's problems instead of waiting for one to appear.

WILL is the leaf that holds the desire to live our best life and the insistence that such desires are possible for your life.

PERSEVERANCE is the leaf that holds the determination to succeed no matter what oppositions and/ or distractions try to obstruct our progress.

SKILL is the leaf that holds the capacity to learn and grow into the next best version of ourselves by turning inspiration into results.

I began to share this message on platforms and inspire audiences with its deeper meaning. After a few years, I decided to ask my grandmother where this message came from. To my surprise, it was my great grandfather Jonathon Cecil Rhoden (my maternal Grandfather's Dad). He was a headmaster in Jamaica West Indies, which is equivalent to a principal here in America. My grandmother happened to be one of his students and she remembers that each morning he would gather the children together on top of the building every morning for assemblies. As a part of their daily routine, he would have them repeat affirmations. Can you believe that at 92 years old when I posed this question to my grandmother she could still remember close to 10 of them? That's over nine decades on this planet! Those seeds that were planted in her as a young child took root and she was able to share them over nine decades with her family. How amazing is that? After that revelation, I immediately started the process of protecting my family's legacy with my intellectual property attorney and registered the following trademarks **COURAGE AND WILL PERSEVERANCE AND SKILL® THE FOUR LEAVES OF LUCK'S CLOVER® & CREATE YOUR OWN LUCK®**

The reality globally is that 90% of our global population are waiting for a "stroke of good luck" to magically drop in their lap! Only 10% of people are truly willing to do the work necessary to live their best life. **The reality is, CREATE it!** You can **CREATE YOUR OWN LUCK®** and unlock your own Four-Leaf Clover.

Will the road be easy? Absolutely not, but is it possible to create new realities and new opportunities for the legacy we will leave on the planet? The answer is **ABSOLUTELY YES!!!**

The fulfillment of our destiny relies on the discovery, development and the deliverance of our goals and dreams. What I know for sure is that I meet so many entrepreneurs that get frustrated along the path of their journey. Sometimes the road ahead can look daunting and maybe even impossible. From experience I can tell you that even when you can't see the completed puzzle, just know your **ACTION** creates the pieces of the puzzle that will fall right into place. We just can't quit before our blessing. Stay the course! Luck is not just when opportunity and preparation meet, Luck is creating the opportunity you have been preparing for.

#EntrepreneurSidebar

THE WAY YOU DO…

As you are creating that next best version of yourself, be confident that no one else has a duplicate assignment. While many people may do something similar to you No one can do what you do, they way you do! The fulfillment of your divine assignment is just as unique as your thumbprint. There are people who are pre-destined to work with you and will only hear your voice, buy your product or enroll in your services.

I spent too many years holding back all of what I had to offer because I thought too many people were doing the same thing. "You have to give the people what they want!" as my friend Linda Clemmons would say. That is what people invest in, the ability to experience more of YOU! Decide today to create more opportunities to monetize and share more of YOU because No one can do what you do, they way you do!

#FaithpreneurFootnote:

" I can do all things through Christ which strengtheneth me. For God shall supply all your needs according to his riches by Christ Jesus." Philippians 4:13 & 19 KJV

"For God hath not given us the spirit of fear; but of power, and of love, and of a sound mind." 2 Timothy 1:7

Fear is the enemy's weapon. He tries to use it to distract us from the fact that we never have to worry because God always has the final say. The devil's goal is to get into our head to plant seeds of fear & doubt. He can't win unless we give him an opportunity to take up residence in our mind. We can't worry and believe in the same breath. If we believe God's word to be true then we live in FAITH not fear. He said that we can do ALL not some things. God's word will never return until him void.

When you feel fear trying to distract you from taking the next step, remember our battle cry "**ACTION ACTION... DESPITE THE DISTRACTION!!**" and keep moving!

Take a few moments to capture your "#ACTIONNOTES" below:

MY PRAYER OF GRATITUDE & INTENTION...:

_____

_____

_____

_____

_____

_____

THE LESSON FOR ME IS...:

_____

_____

_____

_____

_____

_____

MY IMMEDIATE ACTION DESPITE THE DISTRACTION OF FEAR WILL BE TO:

_____

_____

_____

_____

_____

_____

MY STRETCH GOAL...

_____

_____

_____

_____

_____

_____

Remember to share your takeaways with us at:
Facebook:/DestinyDesignU

Twitter:@DestinyDesignU @StacieNCGrant

Instagram: @DestinyDesignU @StacieNCGrant.

DISTRACTION
ALERT

Ego

I have heard many describe EGO as "Edging God Out". Webster's dictionary definition says it's the opinion that you have about yourself. Resist the temptation to believe that you are fabulous all by yourself. Humbly acknowledge where your gifting and talents come from as well as the people who have helped to positively influence your life. Don't believe the hype. Never allow your ego to stifle your growth and stunt your success.

LIFE LESSON 6

COLLABORATION VS. COMPETITION IS THE SECRET TO SUCCESS

When you are confident in your gifting, other people's talents do not intimidate you. You are actually inspired by them. After all, iron sharpens iron. We live in a society where most people enjoy focusing on a win-lose model of behavior rather than a win-win model of behavior. I believe we can build more opportunities for everyone to win if we worked together. Collaborative achievement driven relationships yield more than competitive divisive competition, especially in business.

It is easy for our ego to deceive us in believing that we don't need the help or support of others to succeed. When in actuality we can grow faster and wider working with a team. Entrepreneurs that desire longevity have to be careful not to function with a solopreneur mindset. If you are the only one that can provide the product or service you offer, you limit your options to grow and expand. As I reflect on my early days, I would have spent more time building my team.

Through collaboration, you can maximize your efforts and double your return on both time and financial investments. We can see the benefits even in corporate arena with collaborations like Dunkin Donuts & Baskin Robins, Kinkos & Federal Express and EBay & PayPal to name a few.

To this end, I developed my own Power Team. Dr. Dennis Kimbro said it best; "If you are the smartest person in your group you need a new group." It's not about you being the shining star, it's about who you can learn from that can contribute to making you shine brighter.

For my Destiny Designers University, I developed our **DDU ASSEST INVENTORY ANALYSIS** to help you design your own **Power Team.**

Before you build your **Power Team** you should take inventory on yourself so you can be clear about who would complement your skill set. Writing it out will make it easier to compare and contrast as you make decisions on how to add to your **Power Team**. This is what I refer to as your **P.S.H.** Describe yours below:

Personality Traits (i.e. task oriented, fun loving, dependable, adventurous, analytical etc.)

_____

_____

_____

_____

_____

_____

Soft Skills (i.e. ability to work with a team, communication skills, problem solving skills, etc.)

_____

_____

_____

_____

_____

_____

Hard Skills (i.e. typing, web design, earned degree, certifications, etc.)

_____

_____

_____

_____

_____

_____

You can also ask your team members to complete this same assessment.

The next step is to assess who and what you have access to you in your network. Some of the people you need, you already know and they are willing to help you. Others you may desire to work with because of their level of mastery. This is what I call your **E.R.S.** Describe yours below:

Experts (What industry experts do you know or would you like that have the expertise that would complement your Power Team)

_____

_____

_____

_____

_____

_____

Resources (What resources do you or the people you know have access to like venues, media partners, publicists, attorneys, etc.)

_____

_____

_____

_____

_____

_____

Systems (What systems could help you automate and expand your reach? etc.)

_____

_____

_____

_____

_____

_____

After you analyze your entries, you can then develop a job description for the individuals you need to invite to be on your Power Team. Create projections of who you will need immediately, those who you will need in 3 months and those you will need in 6 months or later.

As you build your team, you have the options of hiring interns or independent contractors, building a sales team, hiring professionals on retainer or hiring employees. When you are first starting out, keep your costs low. Interview interns and independent contractor before putting professionals on retainers or hiring employees. People are willing to get the on the job training experience in exchange for their service. If I could do things all over again, I would have built my sales team first because their commission is based on their productivity. People are motivated to do more if they have the ability to earn more.

#EntrepreneurSidebar

JOINT VENTURES

Your Power Team can also include those who have established brands in your industry. You don't have to compete against your colleagues. Instead you can create joint venture opportunities with people in your industry. For instance, I collaborate with other speakers and trainers at their events where we create a revenue share from anything that I sell. This is a win-win. I get exposed to a new audience and more revenue and my joint venture partner gets to promote my participation/expertise and receive a percentage of the income I generate. Find those who are in alignment with your brand and form mutually beneficial joint ventures.

#FaithpreneurFootnote:

"Be kindly affectioned one to another with brotherly love; in honor preferring one another, Not slothful in business; fervent in spirit; serving the Lord."
Romans 12:10-11

My journey to here has been far from perfect. I have had more than my fair share of learning curves (my replacement for the word mistakes). I know from personal experience what it is to feel like a failure when you compare yourself to the success of others. Without knowing the complete story, we are quick to judge ourselves against someone' else's victories without knowing their tribulations. You can't escape the process. We all have to fulfill our divine destiny and that includes a series of learning curves. It was through my collaborations that I was able to expand my bandwidth and shorten my learning curves. Learn to ask for help not because you are weak but because you want to remain strong.

When your ego tries to interrupt your progress remember our battle cry **"ACTION ACTION… DESPITE THE DISTRACTION!!"** and eat some humble pie.

Take a few moments to capture your "#ACTIONNOTES" below:

MY PRAYER OF GRATITUDE & INTENTION…:

_____

_____

_____

_____

_____

_____

THE LESSON FOR ME IS…:

_____

_____

_____

_____

_____

_____

MY IMMEDIATE ACTION DESPITE THE DISTRACTION OF EGO WILL BE TO:

_____

_____

_____

_____

_____

_____

MY STRETCH GOAL...

_____

_____

_____

_____

_____

Remember to share your takeaways with us at:
Facebook:/DestinyDesignU

Twitter:@DestinyDesignU @StacieNCGrant

Instagram: @DestinyDesignU @StacieNCGrant

DISTRACTION
ALERT

Selfishness

There is a thin line between looking out for your best interest and being totally consumed with yourself. The challenge is when all we care about is our selfish interests and don't take the needs of others into consideration, we block our own blessings. There is such a joy in thinking of the needs of others and how we can be of service. The bonus is when you help people get what they want you can't help but to get what you want.

LIFE LESSON 7

THE TRUE SECRET TO SUCCESS IS TO BE OF SERVICE AND ADD VALUE

One of my favorite quotes comes from Mahatma Gandhi *"The best way to find yourself is to lose yourself in the service of others."* It summarizes how I have lived my life. I have literally served my way to the top. As a servant leader, I enjoy helping others and seeing them experience joy. Actually it is in my DNA. I grew up watching my Grandmother, Mother, Aunts & Uncles always giving of themselves and being a blessing to others. Nothing compares to knowing that you have positively impacted someone's life. Maya Angelou said it best *"I've learned that people will forget what you said, people will forget what you did, but people will never forget how you made them feel."*

As an entrepreneur, your goal is to monetize your products and/ or services in a way that adds value to our global marketplace. The more you serve your audience with the best service the more of the marketplace you will command. Let's take the technology giant Google for an example. They weren't the first in the industry but they currently dominate the industry because their business model led with service first. They amassed the majority of the marketplace by giving away quality service. Now there isn't an aspect of technology that they do not influence. The more energy you put into serving with quality the higher your return will be.

I must caution that you can't sow and reap in the same season. Google didn't become the technology giant they are overnight. They sowed good seeds in the marketplace over a period of time before they saw the return. Unlike Google, I wanted to sow and reap in the same season. I wasn't excited about the idea of waiting but there is no way around the organic process of building relationships through service. Today I am reaping the rewards of seeds I sowed over 2 decades ago.

I get concerned when I meet entrepreneurs who think that they can take the marketplace by storm without being willing to serve. There are times when it is in your best interest to volunteer your service. If I weren't willing to volunteer my time in some key situations I would have never received access to some of the platforms I have shared internationally. You don't need to volunteer your services for everything because that would make your business a hobby but use wisdom in deciding when to be of service as an investment in a long-term relationship or future opportunity. I love the way Douglas Adams put it *"To give real service you must add something which cannot be bought or measured with money, and that is sincerity and integrity."* Your work will speak for itself when you add value. Take the time to master your craft; offer the best service and customers will seek you out. Once you establish your standards under promise and over deliver and you will be irresistible!

In addition to the service you give in business, there is the volunteer/community service component you can add to your global footprint.

I am a part of multiple organizations that provide service within the communities where I live and work. If we want to improve the conditions of the world, it starts with improving the conditions in our own back yard first. Seek ways you can increase your value in the marketplace by incorporating community service into your business model. To whom much is given, much is required.

#EntrepreneurSidebar

CREATE OPPORTUNITIES THROUGH SERVICE

It is through serving you add value to any relationship or situation. The bonus is the experience you gain in the process.

For instance, if you wanted to start an event planning company I would encourage you to research an existing company you admire and set up a 15 minute teleconference meeting with the owner. *(Busy people have limited time. WOW them on the phone first before you try to schedule an in person meeting.)* Here is what you would say

"Hello _____, thank you for your time. My name is _____ and I am an aspiring event planner. I did some research and found that you are running one of the top event planning companies in the area. I would be honored to volunteer 2-4 hours in your office or at one of your upcoming events over the next month. I know I could learn so much from you. I am willing to sign any non-disclosure agreements you may require. Thank you for your time and consideration. I look forward to working with you. When can I come in to meet you in person?"

The possibilities are endless with this exchange. Any savvy professional would be open to this win-win opportunity. They get additional support for any current project and/or event and you get the needed experience/insight in building your brand. Additionally as you grow, this becomes an opportunity for collaboration. You can customize this example for whatever industry you are in. The lesson is to find a way to add value through service.

#FaithpreneurFootnote:

"Now unto him that is able to do exceeding abundantly above all that we ask or think, according to the power that worketh in us." Ephesians 3:20 KJV

"I beseech you therefore, brethren, by the mercies of God, that ye present your bodies a living sacrifice, holy, acceptable unto God, which is your reasonable service." Romans 12:1 KJV

When we are in alignment with God's will for our lives we are then able to proceed with confidence. Our life is a life of service when we are living in our purpose. If we are faithful to God he will be faithful to us. Seek to be a blessing in everything you do and you won't be able to stop the blessings that fall on you.

When you start feeling or acting a little selfish remember our battle cry **"ACTION ACTION… DESPITE THE DISTRACTION!!"** and see who you can be of service to today.

> ### Take a few moments to capture your "#ACTIONNOTES" below:

MY PRAYER OF GRATITUDE & INTENTION…:

_____

_____

_____

_____

_____

THE LESSON FOR ME IS…:

_____

_____

_____

_____

_____

_____

MY IMMEDIATE ACTION DESPITE THE DISTRACTION OF SELFISHNESS WILL BE TO:

_____

_____

_____

_____

_____

_____

MY STRETCH GOAL...

_____

_____

_____

_____

_____

_____

Remember to share your takeaways with us at:
Facebook:/DestinyDesignU

Twitter:@DestinyDesignU @StacieNCGrant

Instagram: @DestinyDesignU @StacieNCGrant

BONUS
LIFE LESSON 8

WORDS HAVE POWER

First let me say, that God has a sense of humor. Sometimes we forgot the "aha" moments of our life but God will bring them to our remembrance. This happened to me one day completing some routine tasks in my office. God brought back to my remembrance how I used to emphatically declare to my girlfriends in college that I knew I was going to be successful one day and I didn't want someone to marry me for my money but because he really loved me. Therefore, I wanted to marry someone that I could build from the ground up with so that I would know his love for me was authentic. Well, when I shared this with my husband his response was "thanks to you and your bright declarations we had to struggle longer than necessary". After sharing a good laugh, I started to think about how many other things I have spoken over my life. What else have I spoken into existence? How many times do we say things in passing and forget what we have put out in the universe. Phrases like "I am broke, I will never find a good man I can never trust a woman, I will never get over that." Life has an interesting way of revealing the truth of who we are at the core in our process. Cancel & clear negative self-defeating words from your life. What you speak about you will bring about. SPEAK LIFE over ever step of your journey and watch what you are able to manifest.

Final #EntreprenuerSidebar

KNOW YOUR WORTH

So many emerging, functional and seasoned entrepreneurs continue to watch their finances hemorrhage and still put on a happy face, get dressed and hit the pavement determined to succeed. Meanwhile, they are in so much pain. Frustrated by not being able to show significant revenue from delivering their service or product to the marketplace.

The ability to make financially savvy decisions is one of the best skill sets you can develop as an entrepreneur. The concept of being in business is that you are actually making money and living a financially balanced life. When your finances are challenged or just flat out burning up in flames, you literally become physically sick. Your will to function and desire to keep moving becomes temporarily paralyzed. As an entrepreneur, it is hard to serve people from a creative and authentic space because you are burdened by your financially reality. Clearly entrepreneurs are risk takers and are not afraid of playing full out. The challenge becomes what to do when you have gambled it all and hit $00.00 in your cash flow. It is great to fake it until you make it but at some point you have to face the music. Ignoring increasing debt and lack of resources will not make them magically appear.

I am very familiar with this reality. I had to evaluate where I was falling short and I realized I didn't honor my value. I was so busy trying to be helpful that I was giving away my talent for free. My mentor Les Brown told me something that caused a paradigm shift for how I approached my business. He said *"People beg for what they need and pay for what they want."* No longer could I allow people to take my value for granted.

I know I give extraordinary service and if they couldn't afford it, that was ok. No more discounts or "homie hook ups". Not only could I no longer continue that practice as a sustainable model for me personally, I have a team that depends on me for their survival.

Take time to reevaluate your business model and how you are showing up in the market place. Be coachable and invest in working with the right professional that can get you off life support and create a profitable revenue model.

Final #FaithpreneurFootnote

"Finally, my brethren, be strong in the Lord, and in the power of his might. Put on the whole armour of God, that ye may be able to stand against the wiles of the devil. For we wrestle not against flesh and blood, but against principalities, against powers, against the rulers of the darkness of this world, against spiritual wickedness in high places. Wherefore take unto the whole armour of God, that ye may be able to withstand in the evil day, and having done all, to stand." Ephesians 6:10-13 KJV

As people of FAITH we can see that we are living in the last days and it is incumbent upon us to be lights in this very dark world. This is not time to play church but truly grow deeper in our walk with Christ. Stay the course and know that this is your time to walk in FAITH knowing you have been equipped for the journey. No matter how long it takes, what's for you is for you. Delay doesn't mean denied. Here is another affirmation from my Spiritual Mother to keep you encouraged on your journey.

MY "NEVER AGAIN" LIST

1. **NEVER AGAIN** WILL I CONFESS "I CAN'T": FOR "I CAN DO ALL THINGS THROUGH CHRIST WHICH STRENGTHENETH ME." (PHILIPPIANS 4:13)

2. **NEVER AGAIN** WILL I CONFESS LACK: FOR "MY GOD SHALL SUPPLY ALL MY NEEDS ACCORDING TO HIS RICHES IN GLORY BY CHRIST JESUS." (PHILIPPIANS 4:19)

3. **NEVER AGAIN** WILL I CONFESS FEAR: FOR "GOD HATH NOT GIVEN ME THE SPIRIT OF FEAR, BUT OF POWER AND OF LOVE AND OF A SOUND MIND." (II TIMOTHY 1:7)

4. **NEVER AGAIN** WILL I CONFESS DOUBT AND LACK OF FAITH: FOR "GOD HATH GIVEN TO EVERY MAN THE MEASURE OF FAITH." (ROMANS 12:3)

5. **NEVER AGAIN** WILL I CONFESS WEAKNESS: FOR "THE LORD IS THE STRENGH OF MY LIFE." (PSALM 27:1); AND "THE PEOPLE THAT KNOW THEIR GOD SHALL BE STRONG AND DO EXPLOITS." (DANIEL 11:32)

6. **NEVER AGAIN** WILL I CONFESS SUPREMACY OF SATAN OVER MY LIFE: FOR "GREATER IS HE THAT IS WITHIN ME THAN HE THAT IS IN THE WORLD." (I JOHN 4:4)

7. **NEVER AGAIN** WILL I CONFESS DEFEAT: FOR "GOD ALWAYS CAUSETH ME TO TRIUMPH IN CHRIST JESUS." (II CORINTHIANS 2:14)

8. **NEVER AGAIN** WILL I CONFESS LACK OF WISDOM: FOR "CHRIST JESUS IS MADE UNTO ME WISDOM." (I CORINTHIANS 1:30)

9. **NEVER AGAIN** WILL I CONFESS SICKNESS: FOR "WITH HIS STRIPES I AM HEALED." (ISAIAH 53:5) AND JESUS "HIMSELF TOOK MY INFIRMITIES AND BARE MY SICKNESSES." (MATTHEW 8:17)

10. **NEVER AGAIN** WILL I CONFESS WORRIES AND FRUSTRATION: FOR I AM "CASTING ALL MY CARES UPON HIM WHO CARETH FOR ME." (I PETER 5:7) IN CHRIST I AM CARE-FREE!

11. **NEVER AGAIN** WILL I CONFESS BONDAGE: FOR "WHERE THE SPIRIT OF THE LORD IS, THERE IS LIBERTY." (II CORINTHIANS 3:17) MY BODY IS THE TEMPLE OF THE HOLY SPIRIT.

12. **NEVER AGAIN** WILL I CONFESS CONDEMNATION: FOR "THERE IS THEREFORE NOW NO CONDEMNATION TO THEM WHICH ARE IN CHRIST JESUS." (ROMANS 8:1) I AM IN CHRIST; THEREFORE, I AM FREE FROM CONDEMNATION.

13. **NEVER AGAIN** WILL I CONFESS LONELINESS: FOR JESUS SAID, "LO, I AM WITH YOU ALWAYS, EVEN UNTO THE END OF THE WORLD." (MATTHEW 28:20); AND "I WILL NEVER LEAVE THEE, NOR FORSAKE THEE." (HEBREWS 13:5)

14. **NEVER AGAIN** WILL I CONFESS CURSES AND BAD LUCK: FOR "CHRIST HATH REDEEMED US FROM THE CURSE OF THE LAW, BEING MADE A CURSE FOR US; THAT THE BLESSING OF ABRAHAM MIGHT COME ON THE GENTILES THROUGH JESUS CHRIST; THAT WE MIGHT RECEIVE THE PROMISE OF THE SPIRIT THROUGH FAITH." (GALATIANS 3:13-14)

15. **NEVER AGAIN** WILL I CONFESS DISCONTENT: "FOR I HAVE LEARNED IN WHATEVER STATE (CIRCUMSTANCE) I AM, THEREWITH TO BE CONTENT." (PHILIPPIANS 4:11)

16. **NEVER AGAIN** WILL I CONFESS UNWORTHINESS: "FOR HE HATH MADE HIM TO BE SIN FOR US WHO KNEW NO SIN; THAT WE MIGHT BE MADE THE RIGHTEOUSNESS OF GOD IN HIM." (II CORINTHIANS 5:21)

17. **NEVER AGAIN** WILL I CONFESS CONFUSION: "FOR GOD IS NOT THE AUTHOR OF CONFUSION, BUT OF PEACE." (I CORINTHIANS 14:33); AND "WE HAVE RECEIVED NOT THE SPIRIT OF THE WORLD, BUT THE SPIRIT WHICH IS OF GOD, THAT WE MIGHT KNOW THE THINGS THAT ARE FREELY GIVEN TO US OF GOD." (I CORINTHIANS 2:12)

18. **NEVER AGAIN** WILL I CONFESS PERSECUTION: "FOR IF GOD BE FOR US, WHO CAN BE AGAINST US?" (ROMANS 8:31)

19. **NEVER AGAIN** WILL I CONFESS THE DOMINION OF SIN OVER MY LIFE: BECAUSE "THE LAW OF THE SPIRIT OF LIFE IN CHRIST JESUS HATH MADE ME FREE FROM THE LAW OF SIN AND DEATH." (ROMANS 8:2): AND "AS FAR AS THE EAST IS FROM THE WEST, SO FAR HATH HE REMOVED OUR TRANSGRESSIONS FROM US." (PSALM 103:12)

20. **NEVER AGAIN** WILL I CONFESS INSECURITY: BECAUSE "WHEN THOU LIEST DOWN THOU SHALT NOT BE AFRAID; YEA THOU SHALT LIE DOWN AND THY SLEEP SHALL BE SWEET...FOR THE LORD SHALL BE THY CONFIDENCE, AND SHALL KEEP THY FOOT FROM BEING TAKEN." (PROVERBS 3:24-26)

21. **NEVER AGAIN** WILL I CONFESS FAILURE: BECAUSE "NAY, IN ALL THESE THINGS WE ARE MORE THAN CONQUERORS THROUGH HIM THAT LOVED US." (ROMANS 8:37)

22. **NEVER AGAIN** WILL I CONFESS FRUSTRATION: FOR "THOU WILL KEEP HIM IN PERFECT PEACE, WHOSE MIND IS STAYED ON THEE BECAUSE HE TRUSTETH IN THEE." (ISAIAH 26:3)

23. **NEVER AGAIN** WILL I CONFESS FEAR OF THE FUTURE: "BUT AS IT IS WRITTEN, EYE HATH NOT SEEN, NOR EAR HEARD, NEITHER HAVE ENTERED INTO THE HEART OF MAN THE THINGS WHICH GOD HATH PREPARED FOR THEM THAT LOVE HIM, BUT GOD HATH REVEALED THEM UNTO US BY HIS SPIRIT." (I CORINTHIANS 2:9-10)

24. **NEVER AGAIN** WILL I CONFESS TROUBLES: BECAUSE JESUS SAID, "IN THE WORLD YOU SHALL HAVE TRIBULATION, BUT BE OF GOOD CHEER; I HAVE OVERCOME THE WORLD." (JOHN 16:33)

Rev. Mother Cora V. Paris

Final "#ACTIONNOTES":

MY PRAYER OF GRATITUDE & INTENTION...:

_____

_____

_____

_____

_____

_____

THE LESSON FOR ME IS...:

_____

_____

_____

_____

_____

_____

MY IMMEDIATE ACTION DESPITE THE DISTRACTION OF NEGATIVE WORDS WILL BE TO:

_____

_____

_____

_____

_____

_____

MY STRETCH GOAL...

_____

_____

_____

_____

_____

_____

Remember to share your takeaways with us at:
Facebook:/DestinyDesignU

Twitter:@DestinyDesignU @StacieNCGrant

Instagram: @DestinyDesignU @StacieNCGrant

I share the following 2 poems with my students in my Destiny Designers® Teen Empowerment Classes for inspiration and I want to leave them with you. The first one President Nelson Mandela used it in his Inauguration speech, but Marianne Williamson wrote it:

"Our deepest fear is not that we are inadequate.
Our deepest fear is that we are powerful beyond measure. It is our light, not our darkness, that most frightens us.

We ask ourselves, who am I to be brilliant, gorgeous, talented, and fabulous? Actually, who are you not to be? You are a child of God.
Your playing small doesn't serve the world.
There's nothing enlightened about shrinking so that other people won't feel insecure around you. We are all meant to shine, as children do.
We are born to make manifest the glory of God that is within us.

It's not just in some of us, it's in everyone.
And as we let our own light shine,
we unconsciously give other
people permission to do the same.
As we are liberated from our own fear,
our presence automatically liberates others."

A Return to Love
Reflections on the Principles of A Course in Miracles by Marianne Williamson

Don't Quit

When things go wrong, as they sometimes will,
When the road you're trudging seems all uphill,

When the funds are low and the debts are high,
And you want to smile, but you have to sigh,

When care is pressing you down a bit-
Rest if you must, but don't you quit.

Life is queer with its twists and turns,
As every one of us sometimes learns,

And many a fellow turns about
When he might have won had he stuck it out.

Don't give up though the pace seems slow -
You may succeed with another blow.

Often the goal is nearer than
It seems to a faint and faltering man;

Often the struggler has given up
When he might have captured the victor's cup;

And he learned too late when the night came down,
How close he was to the golden crown.

Success is failure turned inside out -
The silver tint in the clouds of doubt,

And you never can tell how close you are,
It might be near when it seems afar;

So stick to the fight when you're hardest hit -
It's when things seem worst that YOU MUST NOT QUIT!

Author Unknown

AFTERWORD

YOU WILL BE TRIED BY YOUR TESTIMONY

Publishing these words was no easy feat. I had numerous pieces of the book all over my computer and in my journals for years. When I actually started working on finalizing everything I couldn't believe just how much content I had. I have been carrying this baby for long time but it appeared that it wasn't only post term delivery but it was sitting in a breached position. I had every possible scenario try to block the final production of the book, including the final draft not saving on my computer. All I could do was "Lift my eyes to the hills, from whence cometh my help. My help cometh from the Lord, which made heaven and earth." Psalm 121:1. It got to the point where I almost pushed things back and on the real rough days I felt like throwing in the towel. I had to stop and take a dose of my own medicine: **"ACTION ACTION... DESPITE THE DISTRACTION!!"** I wiped away the tears because you can't worry and pray in the same breath. I prayed, turned on my Gospel playlist, put one foot in front of the other and kept pushing.

I want to thank you from the bottom of my heart for opening your heart and lending me your ears to receive the words of this book . Stay encourage and no matter what keep taking **ACTION ACTION...DESPITE THE DISTRACTION**.

WITH A HEART FILLED WITH GRATITUDE

WARNING: The next few paragraphs contain and overwhelming portion of public admiration so feel free to skip through the rest of these dedications if you cannot tolerate excessive amounts of love at one time.

To my Guardian Angels...

My Pastor/2nd Mother The late Rev. Mother Cora Paris and my Grandmother the late Mrs. Pernell Agatha Rhoden. These two women loved me beyond words and stayed in constant prayer over my life and my submission to God's will for my life. From them I learned the true meaning of FAITH and an authentic Christian journey. My flesh still aches for one more hug, one more kiss and one more conversation but my spirit will remain full of all the lessons they taught me and their legacy will live on in everything I do! These life lessons are a tribute to them.

To my parents ...

A Mother's love is PRICELESS!!! I am so extremely blessed to have had the example of an AMAZING woman as my Mother. My ENTIRE life I watched my Mother stand as a pillar of strength for our nuclear and extended family. She possesses a unique mix of my maternal grandparents; that has given her the ability to love unconditionally and the discipline to lead an army. She has sacrificed so much for her family and my prayer is to always be able to "celebrate her in the gates" as she is TRULY a Proverbs 31 Woman. I love you Mommy more than words could ever express. Thank you for being my first cheerleader, my protector, my advisor, my role model, my angel investor and so much more!! There are no words adequate enough to express my gratitude but I pray you know just how much I LOVE YOU!!!!

Yes, I am still Daddy's little girl. Although I may appear to be the female version of my Daddy, I am the beneficiary of much more than his looks. My Father has always danced to the beat of his own drum and gone where there has been no path and blazed a trail. He has never sought approval from others to live life on his own terms. There is something liberating about owning and standing in your truth. It took me a while to embrace this in my own life but I thank my Dad for always encouraging me to live my truth. I LOVE YOU DADDY to the end of eternity and back.

How many people can celebrate their step-parents? Well I can. My Step-Mother is simply Mom. She has always loved and supported me and we have a special relationship. Mom, thank you for everything and managing my Daddy all these years (smile). I love you and celebrate the incredible woman you are.

I already talked about my maternal Grandmother. Unfortunately, my paternal Grandmother, Agnes Muir died on Mothers Day when my father was 12 years old so I never had the pleasure of meeting her. I have felt her presence in my life (you will read about that & who Coco is in my next book). My Aunt Hyacinth had to raise my Dad and she has been like a grandmother to me. I am grateful for her wisdom, council and support all my life. I treasure our conversations, esp. the ones that kept me encouraged me during the last leg of publishing this book. I love you Aunt Hyacinth and thank God for you and all you mean to our family.

To my in-laws...

My in-laws are more than in-laws. I truly have another set of loving supportive parents, who have blessed me with such an incredible husband. My Mother-in-law had all boys and always longed for her own girl. Now she is blessed to have 2 granddaughters but I am happy to be one of her daughters. Mom, thanks for always being there for me, for your encouragement and advice. Your love and support is priceless. Dad, thank you as well for your love and support.

To my Aunts & Uncles...

How do I adequately express the immeasurable amount of love, encouragement and support I have received from my Aunts & Uncles. My Mother is one of 7 children and I was the fist niece my aunts and uncles were able to share their love with and boy did they. Some would refer to it as spoiling me but I simply refer to it as love. From babysitting me to watching me graduate to starting my own family, they have been there every step of the way. My Uncle Teddy is no longer with us but his love and our secret escapades will be with me forever. Uncle Errol, Aunt P, Aunt Do, Uncle Howie, Aunt G & Uncle Lyndall. I thank you with a full heart of gratitude for all you did to shape the woman I am today. Thank you also to my Auntie Millie, Auntie Bobs, Pat, Al & the entire NJ crew who have loved me since the day I married their nephew/cousin.

I am also fortunate to be extremely close to my maternal Grand Uncle & Grand Aunt who have been with me since birth. Uncle Gossett & Aunt Nells I love you more than words can say. Thank you for your unwavering love and support.

To my cousins...

Well what can I say about all of you crumb snatchers...LOL. Just joking. You know I love each of you and I appreciate you all allowing me to boss you around from my position in the garbage all these years (internal family joke). We are blessed to share a rich legacy from our Grandmother and look forward to sharing our stories to the next generation. To my big "cousins-brothers" Chris & Wally, you balanced me out with learning how to be cool under pressure from one of you and how to be fearless after being terrorized by the other …LOL. Thank you all for loving me unconditionally : Sharon, Joan, Jamie, Jonas, Breanaa, Jonathan, Kadesh, Natasha, George, Jennifer, Lurissa, Ramona, Jonda, Ashley, CJ, Askale, Andrew, Carlotta, Miriam, Nicole, Aaron, Christina, Tiffany, Chantel, Charis, Micah, Kara, Jazmine, Cyree, Joshua, Jabbaari, Jaron, Jiana, Jace, Jakob, Joshua, Jalani, Jamaria, Jamarion, Niyah, Jaquan, Jordan, Araiah, Amari, Alim, Kyle, Cheryl, Marilyn, Alexandria, Kobe & Olivia.

To my husband...

Where do I begin to thank the man I married over 20 years ago. I'll never forget how my heart felt when he proposed to me that rainy night in his Nissan Altima. As best friends turned married couple my life with my husband has been an AMAZING journey of love, laughs, lessons, growth, challenges, faith and memories. There are no words to express how blessed I am to have someone who always puts my needs first and loves & supports me unconditionally. The love we share sometimes feels like a fairytale but this is our life. Our children could have no better example of what being a hard working, principled man of God is. Honey, I LOVE YOU with every fiber of my being and am eternally grateful for the blessing of you in my life. Thank you for being my "supporter-n-chief" in getting this project done.

To my children...

Josiah and Jeremy my young princes, being your mother has been the greatest joy and hardest job of my life wrapped in one. God chose me to deliver the two of you in the world – what an honor!! From the day you both were born, I never knew I could feel a love so all consuming as being a mother. You both continue to teach me quite a bit about myself. As I learn to appreciate your uniquely different personalities and journeys, one thing will always remain the same…NO ONE can love you like I do. Thank you also for supporting me in all my endeavors as you will be the beneficiaries of legacy. Mommy LOVES you both more than you will ever know.

To my sisters...

My big sister Rosanna has always been the cool one that I wanted to be like. We share memories of escapades our parents still don't know about. I am so proud of the mother she is to my amazing niece and the incredible life she worked hard to create. I love her so much and I am grateful to God for sparing her life after a massive stroke a few years ago. Recovery is a process but I'm grateful for the amazing progress you have already made. You gave me the inspiration to complete this book. I love you so much Rosanna and we will be dancing together at Zanneisha's wedding.

My baby sister Danielle is more like my first child with 14 years separating us. She hated feeling like our relationship was more parental in her formative years but I had to help my Mom manage the situation...LOL. Well we have grown up to be inseparable and I am so proud of the woman and mother she has become. Plus, she gave me my two little pumpkins Arielle & Maddison , so she can do no wrong now. Thank you for always having my back and being one of my fiercest protectors. I love you more than words can say Danielle aka Putus!

Novalee having you join our family was a blessing. I am so proud of you and the woman, wife and mother you have become. Thank you for your unwavering love and support.

To my brothers...

Well I have 7 brothers (3 siblings – Chris, Jahwanza, & Ademola and 4 brother in-laws – Fitz, Boris, Hobart & Marcus) and I love them all. All of my brothers have such distinct and different personalities but I appreciate each of them for who they are. One things for sure, I wouldn't advise anyone messing with me because all of them are not 100% sane...LOL. Out of the 7, only 4 are married and my prayer for them is raise their families in the love of Christ and being outstanding role models for their nieces and nephews. I love you all my 4 sister-in-laws; Raziya, Stephanie, Mishawna & Crystal to the moon and back and appreciate your unwavering love and support.

To my nieces, nephews and Godchildren...

Who is a better Auntie – NO ONE …LOL. My nieces, nephews & Godchildren are the joy of my life. I love each of them so much and expect nothing but great things from each of them. I pray that in addition to learning the lessons I share in this book they will be able to share it with the next generations of our family. As long as God gives me breath, I will always be here for my babies and let you get away with our secrets …wink wink. Auntie loves you all: Zanneisha, Tabari, Dandrea, Dylan, Tabar, Jr., Arielle, Maddison, Chyann, Kayla & Lee-Anna, Sharena, Zynaudra, Nigel, Sirobea, Khali, Malani, Daquan, Nazaya, Jiani, Jahbril, Kierra, Nia Adell, Gregory, Latifah, Celisha, Remi, Isaiah, Nia Denae, Reina, Chuckie, Christian, Taylor, Chase, Nye, Evan, Chance, Journey, Azana, Najah, & Autumn, Kayla, Ethan, Jaxon & Jordyn.

To my Pastor & Church Family...

Rev. Gloria Washington who knew when we were growing up together that God would call you to carry on the ministry of your Mother. What a blessing it has been over the last 7 years, to witness the anointing on your life and your continuous growth in the service of the Lord. Thank you for your example of a life dedicated to God's will.

#MyChurchFamilyIsTheBest Thank you to my entire Church family for keeping me lifted up in prayers for my entire life. A special debt of love to Sis. Merivs, Sis. Betty, Sis. Willie, Sis. Christina, Sis. Gracie , Bro. Jonathon & Sis. BobbieAnn.

To Ms. Taur Orange and my ALP Family...

As a teenager I was fortunate enough to be a part of the leadership program that had a huge impact on my leadership and service today. ALP provided me with intensive leadership development training, civic engagement, cultural history and pride that has shaped my view of the world and my commitment to making this world better than I found it. I met one of my greatest role models through this program; Ms. Taur Orange. Ms. Orange thank you for your belief in me, your unwavering support and example of excellence in my life! I love you more than words can say. To all my ALP Family, esp. Group 10, thank you for being a part of some of the best memories of my life. Monica, Mitzi, Jo, John, Andrea, Charon, Royce & Teddy thank you for always having my back.

To my Sorors of Zeta Phi Beta Sorority, Inc.

On June 3, 1989, I joined the greatest sorority on the planet – Zeta Phi Beta Sorority, Inc. in the Outrageous OA Chapter with my sisters for life; Michelle G., Peggy, Harriett, MaryAnn Tara, & Michelle W. There are no words to describe the inseparable bond we share and my love for them. Sorority life is more than colors, signs and calls. It is sacred bond sealed in love and sustained by scholarship and service. Over these almost 3 decades, I have been blessed with the most AMAZING Sorors. I can't list them all but my world not be complete without my OA Babies, PZZ Phoenixes, and my ride or die crew Jodi, Rebecca, Shawana, April, Debbie, Ebony, Juice, Kimberly, Monica, Stephanie, Gigi, April, Stanyell & Diana.

To my other Sisters and Brothers

To my Sisters from another mother: Sonia, Collette, Bridget, Robbie, Donna, Susan, Danessa, DNicole, Carla, DeAnn, Ludy, Shonyea and my brothers from another mother: Rodney, Kamal, Donovan, Roger, Patrick, Kirby, Barry, John & Ronald thank you for your unconditional love and support. Love you to life! A special thank you to the entire Warren family.

To my Sisters of Jack & Jill of America, Inc.

My JJ Sisters are simply amazing and our children outstanding young leaders. It is a joy to live, work and play together. To my sisters in the Queens Chapter, thank you for your love and support. My COSMOPOLITAN Teens, continue to make me proud. I love you all to the moon and back.

To my St. John's University Alumni Network...

Nothing will ever compare to my Undergraduate experience at St. John's University. Both my academic and extra-curricular activities were rewarding and the relationships have lasted a lifetime.

To my Boy Scout Family, Rosedale Jets & Holy Cross Family...

One of the unexpected blessings of parenthood are the relationships you gain as a result of your children's extra-curricular activities. I am blessed to have met some of the most incredible people as a result. Pack & Troop 263 thank you for your love and support. I am so proud of all our young men, especially our 12 Eagle Scouts since 2011 and our Eagle Mom Club.

To my Rosedale Jets Football family, thank you for your love and support. My boys forced me to learn about and subsequently enjoy the game of football. To all our athletes, coaches, & team Moms… #OneTeamOneSound.

My sister Sabena from another mother – Queen of the Holy Cross HS Football Moms, love you to life! All my other sons from the class of 2015 continue to make me proud.

To Susan Taylor and my National Cares Family ...

Since High School when I was exposed to the *In The Spirit* Column in Essence Magazine, I fell in love with the wisdom, authenticity, and passion from the words Susan L. Taylor shared each month.

She was a mentor in my head for years. Now years later I get to call her a friend, confidant and leader in the movement to save our children through the National Cares Mentoring Movement (www.caresmentoring.org). As a part of my volunteer service, I am one of the co-chairs for the QueensNYC Cares Affiliate of NCMM. A portion from the sales of this book will go to QueensNYC Cares Affiliate to support the work of finding mentors for the most vulnerable among us…our children. Thank you Mama Susan for your example of empathy and excellence.

To my colleagues whom I consider family...

I have been humbly blessed to have some amazing people in my FRONT ROW. Thank you all for loving me, stretching me, inspiring me and supporting me. I love you all more than words can say… Les, George, Vera, Linda, Joel, Emma, Jewel, Randall, Lethia, Ruben, Val, Dwight, Wade, Andy, Cassandra, Vince, TC, Tiana, Lucinda, Cheryl, Toni C.B. , Darlene, Monikah, Amy, Robert, Pam, Dee, Pasha, Turiya, Che, Trevor, Dakesha, Lisa Nicole, Star, Julie, Tamika, Necole, Miko, DejaVu, Bershawn, Jason, Devin, LT, Julia, Princess, Anthony, James, Patrick & Henry.

To my clients who have become family...

C&G Enterprises is my company that provides Event Strategies for community based and not-for- profit organizations. Over the years of working with the following organizations, they have become extended family; Sister to Sister International, Inc., Eagle Academy Foundation, Inc. & Mentoring in Medicine, Inc. Thank you David, Kima, Donald, Roger, Susan, Cheryl, Andrew & Lynne for your love & support.

Destiny Designers University® is equally as proud and blessed by the partnerships we have been able to establish with The Women's Academy of Excellence, Macy*s, FraserNet Power Networking Conference, "Women in the Black, Women Doing it Big Foundation", and St. John's University.

ABOUT THE AUTHOR

Dr. Stacie N.C. Grant is living her divine calling to LEAD, TEACH and INSPIRE! Described as "God's Designer Original", she ignites her audiences with her captivating smile, intoxicating humor and boundless energy.

Dr. Grant is a highly sought after international speaker, author, trainer, human relations expert and mistress-of-ceremonies. The strategic focus of Dr. Grant's empowerment platform is executed through her Destiny Designers University®, **"A CLASSROOM WITHOUT BORDERS; WHERE WE GRADUATE TO THE NEXT BEST VERSION OF OURSELVES BY TURNING INSPIRATION INTO RESULTS!"** This multi-media platform provides training in the areas Life Skills, Personal Growth, Leadership and Presentation Skills; with a focus on a work readiness and an entrepreneur success curriculum. As a result of the training received, this community of Destiny Designers® create behavioral shifts in their productivity! Results are measured through their ability to identify and purge the distractions in their lives so they can use what God has already given them to take immediate ACTION on their goals and dreams. Additionally, her Destiny Designers Teen Empowerment Series® provides soft skills and life skills training for High School Scholars that will cultivate, independent critical thinking, positive self-esteem, clear and concise communication skills and a sense of community.

This work is executed through her media platform, virtual classes, and new book release of *"Action Action Despite The Distraction…7 Life Lessons to Thrive & Live Your Destiny Now!"*. She has hosted the popular Monday Mid-Day Motivation show entitled "Create Your Own

Luck with Stacie N.C. Grant" and the TV Pilot "Destiny Designers TV". Additionally, she is a featured speaker for the Rainbow PUSH Wall Street Summit, FrasetNet Annual Networking Conference, NYC Department of Corrections, Bronx Community College, St. John's University, Project Enterprise, Mary J. Blige FFAWN Foundation, Women's Academy of Excellence, The 1209 Affair Success Net Series, Peak Performance Institute, Women Doing It Big Foundation, MACY*S, Celebrity Guest Host for The Network Journal and many more. Dr. Stacie NC Grant also has the distinction of being one of world renowned Les Brown's notable Platinum Speakers, one of his Expert Trainers and the co-host of Les Brown Motivational Monday Night Calls.

As an Entrepreneur, Dr. Grant owns C&G Enterprises an event planning company that provides purpose driven event strategies for community based and not–for–profit organizations. C&G has been featured on Access Hollywood, Fox 5, Metro TV, and WE Television. The event strategies utilized focuses on producing successful outreach events that bring value to the participants and community at large. Annual clients include Mentoring in Medicine, Inc., Sister to Sister International, Inc., St. Paul Community Baptist Church, Inc., Own Your Power Communications, Inc., Achieving Leadership's Purpose, Inc., The Eagle Academy Foundation and Inspired Girls, Inc. Under Ms. Grant's leadership, C&G has received numerous awards, honors and citations from various organizations and government officials for outstanding commitment to excellence in service.

As a Philanthropist, Dr. Grant is the Co-Chair of the Queens NYC Affiliate of the National Cares Mentoring Movement (founded by Susan L. Taylor) whose mission is to recruit, connect and direct mentors to vulnerable young people. Additionally, she is the secretary of her Church Choir, past President of the St. John's University Black Alumni Association, a Life Member of Zeta Phi Beta Sorority, Inc. and Community Service Chair for Jack & Jill of America, Inc. Queens Chapter.

Dr. Grant currently resides in Queens, New York with her husband, Andrew, and 2 sons, Josiah and Jeremy. With God as her guide, our global community will be better for her service to humanity.